## THE HEADSTART BOOK OF
# Looking & Listening

By Shari Lewis and Jacquelyn Reinach

**An important new way
to help children from 2 to 6
develop READINESS for learning.**

Design and Illustration
by Alex and Janet D'Amato

McGRAW-HILL BOOK COMPANY · NEW YORK · LONDON · TORONTO · SYDNEY

# Contents

**H**ERE'S AN IMPORTANT new way to help your child develop *readiness* for all learning. Simple instructions at the beginning of each story show you how your child can participate while you read aloud.

While your child plays along, he develops and improves his basic skills, for each story has been specially designed, under the guidance of leading educators and psychologists, to encourage specific developmental abilities.

The Headstart Book of Looking and Listening will help your child develop his visual and auditory perception:

> Recognizing colors / Telling left from right / Training in eye-hand coordination / Identifying sizes / Identifying shapes / Relating words to the objects they stand for / Listening / Extending attention span / Following directions / Speaking clearly / Hearing differences / Hearing rhymes / Using memory

While some of the stories concentrate particularly on the primary skills of listening, extending attention span and following directions, all of the stories encourage these abilities in addition to the others described.

**Foreword** .............................. 5
   By Dr. Harry S. Gilbert

**How to Use This Book** ...................... 6

**How Do You Do?** ......................... 8
   Telling left from right

**The Little Red Hen** ....................... 12
   Listening; following one direction

**Old Mother Hubbard** ...................... 18
   Relating words to the objects they stand for; using memory; training in general visual perception

**The North Wind and the Sun** ................. 21
   Following directions; training in general auditory perception

**Nimble B. Bimble** ........................ 24
   Listening; extending attention span; speaking clearly

**Under the Rainbow** ....................... 28
   Recognizing colors; hearing rhymes

**Silly Billy** ............................. 33
   Relating words to the objects they stand for; hearing rhymes

**The Blob** .............................. 37
   Identifying shapes; training in eye-hand coordination

**The Market Basket** ....................... 41
   Listening, following complex directions; using memory

**The Pet Shop Mystery** ........................ 45
    Hearing differences in the sounds of words; relating words to the objects they stand for

**Goldilocks** ........................................ 49
    Identifying sizes and shapes

**Handy Andy** ...................................... 55
    Reinforcement in telling left from right

**A Guide to Play Tools for Children** ........... 58

**A Guide to Books for Parents** ................. 60

## Our Thanks
*We would like to thank the countless people whose ideas helped us synthesize the readiness skills and create the play-along technique; especially, Dr. Charles Child Walcutt; Dr. Melvin Schrier and Dr. Sidney Groffman of the Center for Perceptual Development, New York; Mrs. Mildred Rabinow of the Child Study Association of America; and Mrs. Grant Bedell of the Tom Thumb Nursery School, Rye, New York.*

*S. L. and J. R.*

# Foreword

THE MOST RAPID PERIOD of growth in the entire life span occurs during the preschool years. Think of the enormous changes from the helpless newborn to the active, bubbling, talkative, creative kindergarten child!

Skills in doing, thinking, talking, listening, reacting, and socializing are already quite advanced. Psychologists have been aware for a long time that such normal psychological and physical development is essential for the more formal learning of the school years. Yet it is only recently that the general public has become aware of the *necessity* to provide the opportunities for preschool children to attain an all-around satisfactory developmental level if school progress is to be a normal, enjoyable, and successful experience.

Much has been written about the need for giving infants and toddlers emotional security as a basis for developing strong egos and the ability to adapt to an increasingly more complex life. Parents have been deluged with cautions and advice to the extent that many have become bewildered and fearful of making psychological missteps.

In sharp contrast there is very little material available for adults interested in specific ways of helping preschool children to develop skills in listening, knowing, observing, thinking, and imagining. Fortunately in today's climate of understanding the importance of preschool years, two skillful practitioners of the fine art of meaningful play with young children—Shari Lewis and Jacquelyn Reinach—have come along with an excellent series of books. Told in simple, easy-to-follow language and geared obviously to delight and inform preschoolers, these books should be a resourceful mine for parents, teachers, counselors, school aides, and, hopefully, big brothers, sisters, and grandparents.

You may use these books with zest and confidence in your relations with children. With this kind of emotional set, you will be sending your youngsters off to a learning career in fine fettle.

Harry B. Gilbert, Ph.D.
*Member, Board of Examiners,*
*New York City Board of Education*

# How to Use This Book

**For Mother, Father, Grandparents, Teachers, Older Brothers and Sisters, or Baby-Sitters**

In each story your child plays along while you read the story aloud. The directions will be found at the beginning of each story and will look like this:

 This picture will be next to directions for you.

 This picture will be next to the directions for the child playing along. Read these out loud.

Enjoy Headstart story time with your child. These stories are not tests! Give help whenever he needs it, for a happy, successful experience is the best head start of all.

Since children vary so enormously in their rate of development, you may want to use these stories in several ways, depending on how your child responds.

**Your two-and-a-half- or three-year-old** may or may not be ready to participate fully, but would enjoy looking at the pictures and hearing the stories.

**Your nursery school child or first grader** is probably ready to play along but may need to have the directions repeated several times. Or he may enjoy playing along for part of the story and then find it difficult to pay attention.

If this happens, explain the directions to your child again and see if you can renew his interest in the story. If your youngster's attention span has been depleted, put the story away until another day; then start the story from the beginning with all the fresh enthusiasm of a first reading.

**Older children**, who can already read, may strengthen their skills by playing "mother's helper" and reading the stories to younger brothers and sisters (or taking turns and reading to *you* while you play along).

After you have read these stories in their simplest play-along version, you and your child may enjoy the challenge of more advanced games that can be played with each story. "More Ways to Play Along" will be found at the end of each story.

Telling left from right
# How to Play Along

 Every time you come to the phrase "How do you do" and the 🔴 , stop and wait for your child to shake right hands with you. Help him remember by showing him how to fit his hand into the picture on the preceding page. For a very young child, extend your hand first as you are reading and touch his right hand.

 Here's a poem about Noah greeting all the animals as they come aboard the ark. Can you be Noah? Everytime you hear the words "How do you do," shake hands with me with your right hand. If you have any trouble remembering your right hand, it's the hand that fits into the picture on the preceding page.

# How Do You Do?

O<small>NCE UPON A WHILE AGO</small>
When Noah's ark was new,
The animals all came aboard
And lined up, two by two.

And Noah stuck his right hand right out and said:

"HOW DO YOU?" 🔴   to the Doodlebugs,
And "HOW DO YOU DO?" 🔴   to the Sheep,
And "HOW DO YOU DO?" 🔴   to the Kangaroos,
Who hopped aboard with a leap!

9

He said:

"HOW DO YOU DO?" 🛑 to the Elephants
(They shook his hand with their trunks),
And holding a rose to the end of his nose,
He said, "HOW DO YOU DO?" 🛑 to the Skunks!

He said:

"HOW DO YOU DO?" 🛑 to the Hummingbirds,
And "HOW DO YOU DO?" 🛑 to the Bees,
And then to the scariest pair of Bears,
"HOW DO YOU DO? 🛑 , if you please!"

He said:

"HOW DO YOU DO?" 🛑 to the Cockatoos,
And then he shook hands with the Hogs,
And ducking the spines of the Porcupines,
Said, "HOW DO YOU DO?" to the Frogs.

He said:

"HOW DO YOU DO?" 🛑 to the Rattlesnakes,
And hollered "Hello" to the Boa.
The animals bowed and then the whole crowd
Said, "HOW DO YOU DO?" 🛑 to Noah!

## More Ways to Play Along

1. Read the poem again. This time, ask your child to say hello by waving his left hand in the air every time he hears "HOW DO YOU DO." Explain that his left hand is his "other" hand—the hand that is "left"!

2. This time, ask your child to shake hands with his right hand and wave his left hand in the air, both at the same time.

Listening; following one direction
# How to Play Along

Whenever you see the sign 🛑 stop and wait for your child to say "NOT I" in a different voice. You might suggest to him that he use a low voice, a normal voice, and a high voice. You might also suggest that he act out each of the animals, using his body and his face, as well as his voice.

Whenever I stop reading, can you say "NOT I"? Listen carefully. Sometimes the Duck will be speaking, sometimes the Mouse, and sometimes the Pig. See if you can say "NOT I" in different funny voices that remind you of these animals. How would the Duck say "NOT I", and the Mouse, and the Pig? Now see if you can remember those voices and use them each time for the same animal.

# The Little Red Hen

One day Little Red Hen was in the farmyard with her chicks looking for something to eat, when she found some grains of wheat.

"I wonder who will help me PLANT this wheat," she said to the other animals on the farm.

The Duck said:　🛑　"_____."
The Mouse said:　🛑　"_____."
The Pig said:　🛑　"_____."

"Then I'll plant the wheat myself," said Little Red Hen. And she did.

When the wheat had grown tall, Little Red Hen said to the other animals on the farm, "Now who will help me CUT this wheat?"

13

The Duck said: 🔴 "_____."
The Mouse said: 🔴 "_____."
The Pig said: 🔴 "_____."

"Then I'll cut the wheat myself," said Little Red Hen. And she did.

When the wheat was cut, Little Red Hen needed someone to help her separate the grain from the stalks.

"I wonder who will help me THRESH this wheat," she said to the other animals on the farm.

The Duck said: "_____."
The Mouse said: "_____."
The Pig said: "_____."

"Then I'll thresh the wheat myself," said Little Red Hen. And she did.

When the wheat was threshed, Little Red Hen said, "Now, who will help me CARRY this heavy bag of wheat to the mill and grind it into flour?"

The Duck said: "_____."
The Mouse said: "_____."
The Pig said: "_____."

"Then I will carry the wheat to the mill, and I will grind it into flour," said Little Red Hen. And she did.

When the wheat was ground into flour, Little Red Hen carried it home and said, "Now who will help me BAKE this bread?"

The Duck said:     "_____."
The Mouse said:    "_____."
The Pig said:      "_____."

"Then I'll bake it myself," said Little Red Hen. And she did.

Soon a wonderful smell of freshly baked bread spread all around the farmyard. Little Red Hen took the crusty loaf out of the oven.

"Now I wonder who will help me EAT the bread," she said to the other animals on the farm.

"I will," quacked the Duck.
"I will," squeaked the Mouse.
"I will," grunted the Pig.

"Oh, no, you won't," cried Little Red Hen. "You did not help me plant or cut or thresh or carry or bake. So you will *NOT* help me eat my bread. My little chicks will help me do that." And they did.

## More Ways to Play Along

1 Read the story again, but mix up the order in which the animals speak. Tell your child that you are going to try to trick him into giving the wrong voices for each animal, and so he should listen very carefully.

2 As you read the story, leave out the words printed in red, but point to the related picture. Ask your child to tell you what Little Red Hen is doing.

# Old Mother Hubbard

**Relating words to the objects they stand for; using memory; training in general visual perception**

## How to Play Along

Read the poem slowly, allowing time for your child to identify the correct pictures. After the poem, play this game: Let your child look back at the pictures for one minute. Tell him that you want him to look very carefully at all the things Mother Hubbard bought. Then take the book away and ask him how many of those things he can remember. Keep score and play the game again after another reading.

See if you can find the right pictures as I talk about them in the poem. But listen carefully, because there's a game to play afterward.

O<small>LD  M<small>OTHER</small>  H<small>UBBARD</small></small>
Went to the cupboard
To give her poor Dog a bone.

But when she got there,
The cupboard was bare
And so the poor Dog had none.

18

She went to the butcher's
To buy him a bone,
But when she came back
He was using the phone.

She went to the baker's
To buy him some bread,
But when she came back
He was making the bed.

She went to the market
To buy him some fruit,
But when she came back
He was playing the flute.

She went to the florist's
To buy him a flower,
But when she came back
He was taking a shower.

She bought him a bike
That was nice as could be,
But when she came back
He was watching TV.

She went to the toy store
To buy a balloon.
He took the balloon
And flew off to the moon!

## More Ways to Play Along

1 When your child can remember five things or more in the game, play again, asking him to recall how many different things the dog was *doing*. Always let him look at the pictures first.

2 Read the poem, but leave out the last line of each verse. See if your child can remember it.

# The North Wind and the Sun

> **Following directions; training in general auditory perception**
>
> ## How to Play Along
>
>  When you see the sign 🟠 stop and wait for your child to blow like the wind or to smile like the sun.
>
>  There are two things to remember in this play-along story. Blow like the wind every time I say the word BLOW. Smile like the sun every time I say the word SMILE.

O<small>NE DAY</small>, up in the sky, the North Wind, a blustery fellow, began to argue with the Sun:

"Who is stronger?
Who is stronger?"
Cried the North Wind to the Sun.
"I am stronger,
And I'll prove it.
You'll see who's the stronger one!"

"There's a lady,
See the lady
Walking down there on the ground.
I will quickly
BLOW 🟥 her coat off,
I'm the strongest thing around!"

21

"BLOW 🟥 and BLOW 🟥,
BLOW 🟥 and BLOW 🟥,"
Howled the Wind with all his might,
But he couldn't
Rip her coat off,
For the lady held on tight.

"Who is stronger?
Who is stronger?
I will show you," said the Sun.
"You may BLOW 🟥, Sir,
But I know, Sir,
I will prove the stronger one."

"Watch me SMILE 🟥, Sir,
Watch me SMILE, Sir,"
And the Sun began to gloat,
For the lady,
Feeling warm, Sir,
Started opening her coat.

Then she quickly
Took her coat off,
As the Sun said with a grin,
"You may BLOW 🟥, Sir,
But I know, Sir,
That a SMILE 🟥 will always win!"

## More Ways to Play Along

1 Read the poem again. This time you pretend to blow or smile instead of saying the words. Ask your child to say the correct word.

2 Discuss the meaning of the story with your child. Perhaps you might like to ask him questions like these:

    **a** Did the North Wind think he was prettier than the Sun? Older than the Sun?

    **b** What did the North Wind think he was strong enough to do to the lady?

    **c** What did the lady do when the North Wind blew? What would you have done?

    **d** Why did the lady take off her coat when the Sun smiled?

    **e** Which do you think is better, howling or smiling when you want something?

# Nimble B. Bimble

**Listening; extending attention span; speaking clearly**

## How to Play Along

The phrases printed in red are tongue twisters. Each is followed by a question. As you read, emphasize the phrases, ask the question, and wait for your child to repeat the tongue twister. Help him if he has difficulty.

This story is about a talking dog. Listen very carefully. I'll be asking questions about what the dog said. Can you answer?

ONCE UPON A TIME there was a very particular, rather unique, somewhat intelligent dog who could *speak!* He would say, "My name is NIMBLE B. BIMBLE." What was his name? (_____)

His little mistress, Thimble B. Bimble, called him Nimble B. Bimble because he had a nimble tongue. When she would say, "Time to get up for breakfast, Nimble B. Bimble," he'd wag his tail and reply, "SERVE ME SIX SAUCERS OF APPLE SAUCE!" What would he reply? (_____)

Sometimes Thimble B. Bimble became angry because Nimble B. Bimble simply refused to act like a dog. If they'd go for a walk, she'd throw a stick and ask him if he'd like to pick it up.

He'd turn up his nose and say, "NO, I'LL ONLY PICK UP THREE TREE TWIGS!" What would he say? (_____)

"Nimble B. Bimble," she'd grumble, "can't you act like a regular dog?" And he would say, "I WOULD IF I COULD, IF I COULD THEN I WOULD." What would he say? (_____)

"Oh, dear," mumbled Thimble B. Bimble, "maybe I might have had more fun with a little goldfish instead of a dog."

"She just doesn't appreciate me!" said Nimble B. Bimble to himself. "I'm finer than a SKINNY, FINNY, FUNNY FISH!" What was he finer than? (_____)

One night Thimble B. Bimble went to the movies, leaving Nimble B. Bimble in charge of the house. For a while, Nimble amused himself by reading the labels on all the packages in the kitchen cabinet. "A BOX OF MIXED BISCUITS WITH A BISCUIT MIXER," he read. What did he read? (_____)

Suddenly he heard someone fumbling with the back door. "Bow-wow," he barked. After all, he *was* a watchdog, and even very particular, rather unique, somewhat intelligent dogs who can speak do bark sometimes.

"Nice doggie," mumbled the man as he stumbled into the kitchen.

Now Nimble B. Bimble was angry. How dared anyone just walk into the house like that! What would Thimble B. Bimble say? So

he bared his teeth, flopped back his ears, and shouted, "YOU'RE A MUMBLING, GRUMBLING, FUMBLING THIEF!" What did he shout? (_____)

"Who said that?" cried the thief. "Dogs can't talk."

Nimble B. Bimble snarled. "Ah, but I am a very particular, rather unique, somewhat intelligent dog who can speak!"

The thief was so surprised, he just stood there, frozen with fright, as Nimble B. Bimble trotted to the telephone, dialed a number with his paw, and said to the operator very politely, "POLICE PRECINCT, PLEASE." What did he say very politely? (_____)

Then Nimble B. Bimble just stood quietly and whistled at the thief until the police arrived.

When Thimble B. Bimble came home, she was so proud of Nimble B. Bimble that she said, "I'll never ask you to be just a regular dog again. For you are a very special spaniel."

And Nimble B. Bimble, being a very particular, rather unique, somewhat intelligent dog who could speak, merely smiled and said, "FORSOOTH, THAT'S THE TRUTH." What did he say? (_____)

## More Ways to Play Along

1. Read the story again. Ask your child to repeat each phrase quickly two times in a row; then three times in a row.

2. Here are some more tongue twisters. See if your child can say them:
   a) Rubber buggy bumper.
   b) She sells seashells on the seashore.
   c) A big black bug bit a big blue bear.

Recognizing colors; hearing rhymes
## How to Play Along

When you see the 🛑 , stop and wait for your child to point to the correct picture.

Every time I stop, see if you can point to the picture I've just mentioned.

# Under the Rainbow

JUST UNDER THE RAINBOW there lived a Queen, known affectionately to all her subjects as Geraldine, the GREEN QUEEN 🛑 . Yes, she was a beautiful greeny green, like grass in the springtime when the sun shines on it.

Every morning the GREEN QUEEN 🛑 would practice on her YELLOW CELLO 🛑 . When she was finished, she would place her BROWN CROWN 🛑 neatly on her head and call her favorite pet, Drew, the BLUE KANGAROO 🛑 . Drew was a soft, bluey blue, like the sky in summer.

Then they would ring for breakfast, which always came to the table on a GRAY TRAY 🛑 . This particular morning the GREEN QUEEN 🛑 leaned over the GRAY TRAY 🛑 and took two slices of RED BREAD 🛑 , a bottle of cherry-flavored milk, which was her favorite PINK DRINK 🛑 , and two ORANGE ORANGES 🛑 , which she shared with Drew, the BLUE KANGAROO 🛑 .

29

As they were eating, a group of visitors wandered into the palace dining room by mistake. They took one look at the GREEN QUEEN ⬢ sitting across the table from the BLUE KANGAROO ⬢ and burst out laughing. "Ha, ha," they cried, "what funny-looking colors you are!"

The Queen, who was wise as well as green, didn't mind the laughter of her rude guests. Smiling sweetly, she said, "Good morning. I expect that you are laughing at Drew and me because we look strange to you. But here in the Land under the Rainbow everything is brightly colored—red, green, brown, yellow, pink."

"And blue," chimed Drew, who was, after all, the BLUE KANGAROO ⬢

"In fact," continued the Queen, as two tears spilled down her green nose, "it must be terrible to have to look at the same old color on everybody and everything day in and day out. How very unlovely!"

As the visitors listened to the Queen, they stopped laughing, and soon tears began to spill down their all-the-same-colored noses. "Well, now, don't cry," said the Queen. "You can't help it if you don't come in rainbow colors, as we do."

Then Geraldine, the GREEN QUEEN ⬢ invited the visitors to share her picnic breakfast. She called for more RED BREAD ⬢ and another bottle of the PINK DRINK ⬢ . She even played a song on her YELLOW CELLO ⬢ . Soon the visitors were laughing and enjoying all the wonderful colors around them.

They knew they would remember their visit to the Land under the Rainbow for a long, long time.

## More Ways to Play Along

**1** Read the story again, name the color, but leave out the name of the object. Ask your child to find the right picture and tell you the name of the object. For example, "Every morning Geraldine, the Green _____." Wait for your child to find the picture that is green and identify the "green queen."

**2** Do the opposite of the above. Leave out the name of the color. Ask your child to point to the picture and tell you the color. For example, "Every morning Geraldine, the _____ Queen." Ask your child, "What color Queen?" and wait for him to tell you "green queen."

**3** Play the Colors Game: Ask your child to close his eyes. Then help him point to a familiar object in the room. Ask him to tell you the color of the object, and then see how many things he can think of that are of that color.

Relating words to the objects they stand for; hearing rhymes

## How to Play Along

As you read, follow the story with your finger. When you come to a word printed in red, shout it out. When you reach a blank space, calling for a rhyming word, show your child the three pictures next to the space. Ask him to name the three objects and choose the word that rhymes.

Every time I stop reading, I'm going to leave out a word. Can you find the picture that stands for the missing word? The end of that word will sound like a word that I just shouted. It will rhyme.

I saw a cat
In Daddy's

The right picture is hat. Doesn't the end of "hat" sound just like "cat"?

# Silly Billy

AT BEDTIME every single night
A little boy named Billy
Always made an awful fuss,
He acted very silly.

Guess
what
he
would
do?

33

He
would
Jump up and DOWN
like a circus _____.

Hiss and SPAT
like a big black _____.

Prance and JIG
Like a dancing _____.

Shiver and SHAKE
Like a wiggly _____.

Holler and HOWL
Like an angry _____.

"Stop it, Billy!" cried his Mom.
"Stop it," said his Dad,
"Get into bed this minute
"'Cause you're being very bad."

"But I have to stamp! I have to yell,
I have to!" Billy said,
"Because, because, because there is
A dragon in my bed!"

Dad said, "Of course! But why the fuss?
How lucky can you get?
Now if I had that dragon,
I would keep him for a pet!"

Billy thought
and
thought
and
decided
not
to
Jump up and DOWN
Like a circus _____,

Hiss and SPAT
Like a big black _____,

Prance and JIG
Like a dancing _____,

Shiver and SHAKE
Like a wiggly _____,

Holler and HOWL
Like an angry _____.

Do
you
know
what
he
did?

He ran into his bedroom
And he named his dragon "Dwight."
Now Billy gets to bed on time
Every single night!

And so does Dwight.

## More Ways to Play Along

1 Play a find-a-rhyme game with the pairs of rhyming words in the story. For example, start with "Cat" and "Hat." How many other words can your child rhyme such as fat, rat, sat?

2 Try re-reading favorite nursery rhymes, shouting out the first rhyming word and leaving out the second, as you did in "Silly Billy." See if your child can fill in the missing rhyming word. "Seesaw, Margery Daw" and "Humpty Dumpty" are clear and simple.

# The Blob

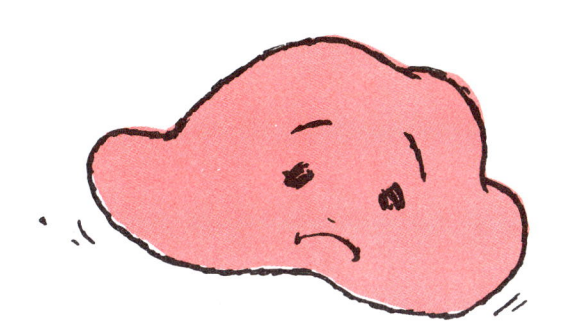

**Identifying shapes; training in eye-hand coordination**

## How to Play Along

Whenever you see the ●, stop and wait for your child to move his finger along the road until he comes to the object you have just named. Then read the verse and ask the question which follows.

In this story a sad little Blob is walking along a road, trying to make new friends. Can you walk with him? As I tell the story, move your finger along the road. Stop when the Blob stops. Move when the Blob walks. Look carefully, because I'm going to ask some questions.

There was a Blob who was a glob
Of nothing much at all.
He wasn't exactly short or wide
Or thin or fat or tall,

Or little or flat or big or huge
Or anything you might see;
A kind of a quiet, rather sad, and
Lonely Blob was he.

One day the Blob went walking down the road hoping to find a friend. He met a round BALL ●, and he stopped.

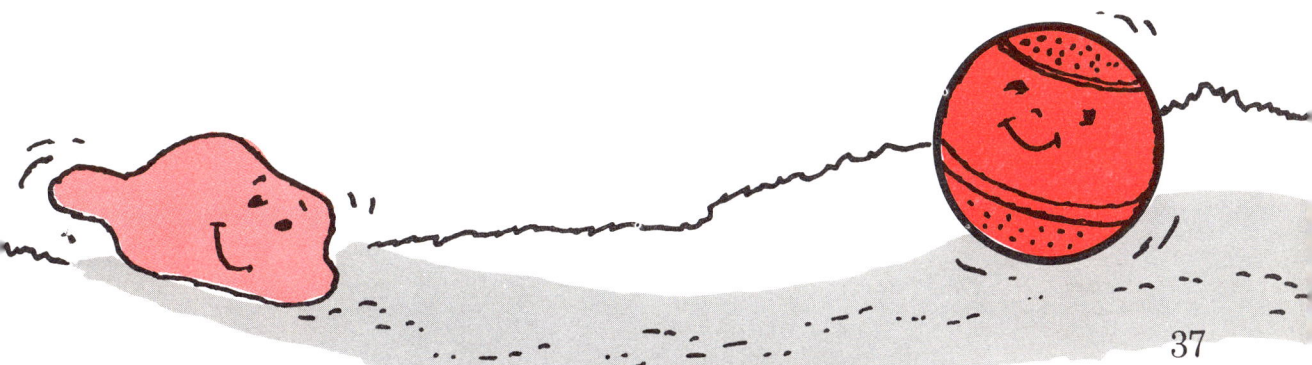

37

"Play with me?"
Said the Blob to the ball.
"I'm lonely as I can be!"
The red ball frowned,
"If you're not round,
Then you can't play with me!"

Was the Blob round? _____ (no)

The Blob sobbed and started walking again. Next he met a square BLOCK 🔴 , and he stopped.

"Play with me?"
Said the Blob to the block.
"I'm lonely as I can be!"
Said the block, "Beware,
If you're not square,
Then you can't play with me!"

Was the Blob square? _____ (no)

So once again the Blob walked down the road. He met a sailboat, whose sail was a three-cornered shape like a TRIANGLE 🔴, and he stopped.

"Play with me?"
Said the Blob to the boat.
"I'm lonely as I can be!"

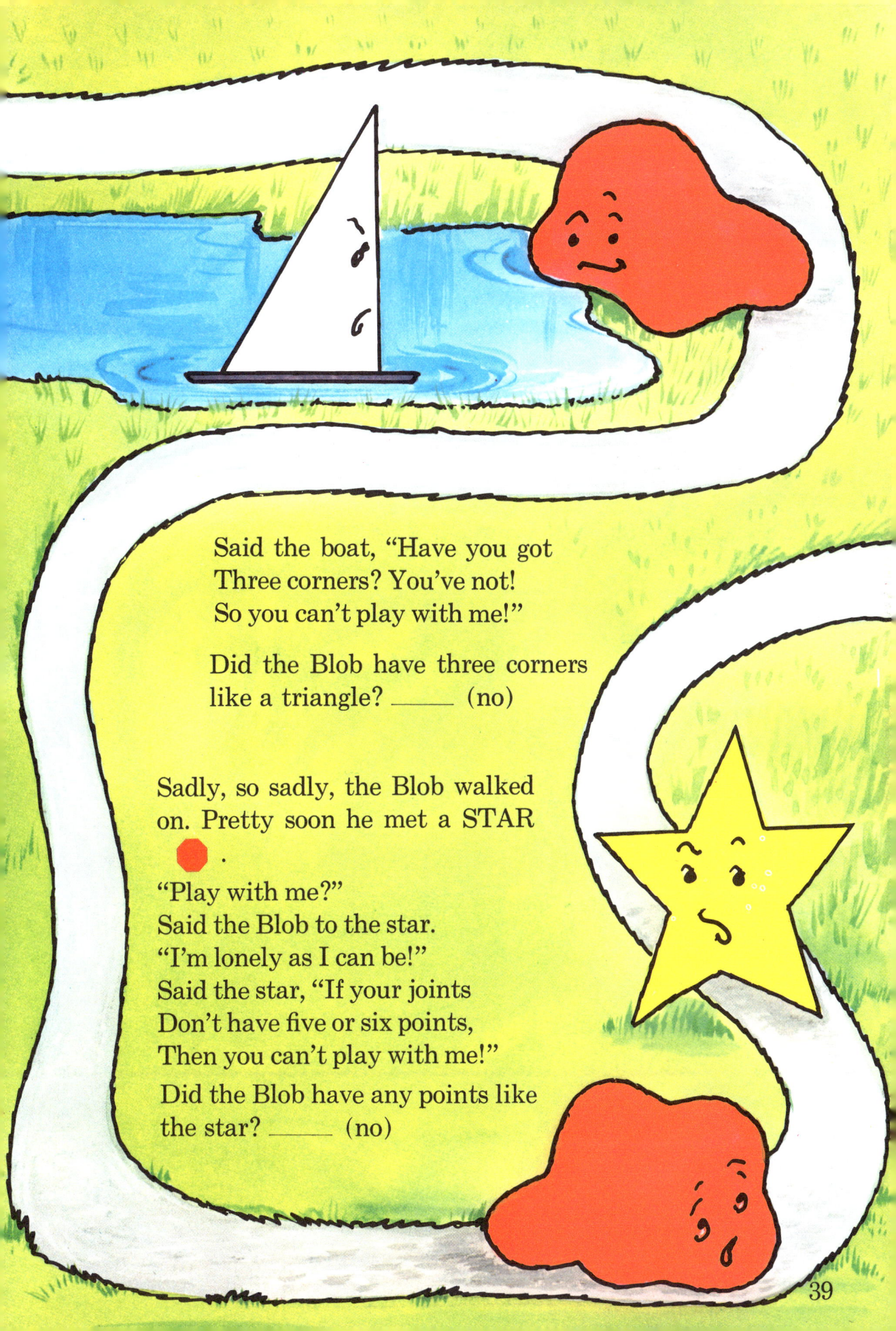

Said the boat, "Have you got
Three corners? You've not!
So you can't play with me!"

Did the Blob have three corners
like a triangle? _____ (no)

Sadly, so sadly, the Blob walked on. Pretty soon he met a STAR 🟥.

"Play with me?"
Said the Blob to the star.
"I'm lonely as I can be!"
Said the star, "If your joints
Don't have five or six points,
Then you can't play with me!"

Did the Blob have any points like
the star? _____ (no)

So the Blob kept walking and walking, and whom do you think he met next ⬢ ?

Another Blob who was a glob
Of nothing much at all,
Who wasn't exactly short or wide
Or thin or fat or tall,

Or little or flat or big or huge
Or anything you might see,
Who smiled and giggled and
    happily said,
"Will you be friends with me?"

And what do you think the Blob said? \_\_\_\_ (yes)

## More Ways to Play Along

**1** Ask your child to follow the road with his finger and name the shapes that the Blob meets along the way.

**2** Ask your child to look at the pictures again and show you something round; something in the shape of a triangle; something square; something with five points. What objects can he find in your house with some of these shapes?

# The Market Basket

**Listening, following complex directions; using memory**

## How to Play Along

Every time you see the 🔴, point to your child and see if he can remember the items in Mrs. Smith's shopping cart.

In this story, Anita's mother asks a lot of questions. Listen to the story and see if you can answer for Anita.

It was a very beautiful morning when Anita Smith and her mother went to market.

As they pushed the shopping cart up and down the aisles, Mrs. Smith put on her glasses and consulted her shopping list. "The first thing we need," she said, "is a loaf of bread." So Anita reached up and put a loaf of bread into the basket.

But Mrs. Smith was an absentminded lady. A very absentminded lady. She even had trouble remembering her own name. A moment later she said, "Anita, dear, do you remember what we put in the basket?"

"Yes, Mother," said Anita. "There's a 🔴 _____." (loaf of bread)

"Thank you," said her mother. "Well, then, we had better get three tangerines for lunch." So Anita ran over, picked out three tangerines, and put them in the basket.

41

"Thank you," said her mother. And looking again at her list, she said, "Well, now we need a quart of milk." So Anita carefully put a quart of milk in the basket.

But Mrs. Smith was an absentminded lady. "Anita, dear, do you remember everything we've put in the basket?"

"Yes, Mother," said Anita. "There's a 🛑 _____ and _____ and a _____." (a loaf of bread and three tangerines and a quart of milk)

"Thank you," said her mother. "Now, let's see, we need a pound of string beans." So Anita put a pound of string beans into a paper bag and put them in the basket.

But Mrs. Smith was an absentminded lady. A very absentminded lady. She even had trouble remembering her own name. So a minute later she said, "Anita, dear, do you remember everything that we've put in the basket?"

"Yes, Mother," said Anita. "There's a 🛑 _____ and _____ and a _____ and a ____ ____." (a loaf of bread and three tangerines and a quart of milk, and a pound of string beans)

"Oh, thank you," said her mother. "You really are a wonderful helper."

(If your child has remembered the items so far, go on. If not, stop and reread the story another time until he can do so.)

But halfway home Mrs. Smith wrinkled her brow and scratched her head absentmindedly. "Anita," she said, "I can't remember! How many tangerines did we buy?"

🛑 "_____, Mother," said Anita. (three tangerines)

"And how many quarts of milk did we buy?"

🛑 "_____, Mother," said Anita. (one quart)

"And how many loaves of bread did we buy?"

🛑 "_____, Mother," said Anita. (one loaf)

"And what else did we buy?"

🛑 "_____, Mother," said Anita. (a pound of string beans)

"Oh, thank you," said her mother. "You're a wonderful helper. Really a wonderful helper!"

But as they reached the door of their house, Mrs. Smith wrinkled her brow and scratched her head. "Oh, dear. I've completely forgotten what we bought at the market. Can you remember, Anita?"

Anita said, "Yes. We bought a 🛑 _____ and _____ and a _____ and a _____." (a loaf of bread and three tangerines and a quart of milk and a pound of string beans)

"Oh, thank you," said her mother. "You're a wonderful helper. Really a wonderful helper. But as you know, I'm an absentminded lady. A very absentminded lady. Tell me one more thing. What's my name?"

## More Ways to Play Along

Read the story again, and this time visit other kinds of stores. When you come to the items in the story (which are printed in red), substitute the new items that might be found in the kind of store you're visiting. For example, Mrs. Smith could go to a shoe store and purchase a pair of bedroom slippers, three pairs of socks, fur-lined boots, and black patent leather shoes.

At the hardware store she might fill her basket with a hammer, six very long nails, thumbtacks, and a sharp saw.

At the toy store she could buy a big brown Teddy bear, a pair of roller skates, a dozen marbles, and a set of electric trains.

# The Pet Shop Mystery

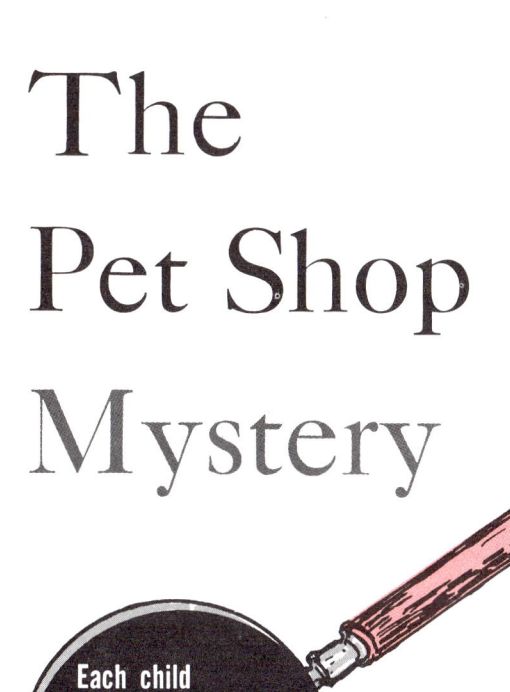

**Each child can buy any animal whose name begins with the same sound his name begins with!**

> Hearing differences in the sounds of words; relating words to the objects they stand for
>
> ## How to Play Along
>
> Read the instructions below, and the clue on this page carefully to your child.
>
> Then turn to the picture mystery on the next page. Read the captions under each picture and wait for your child to find the right animal.
>
> Help a very young child by filling in the name for him and asking him to find the picture.
>
> This is a picture mystery. The children on the next page can't find the animals they want to buy. Can you help them? Listen to the clue and then see if you can be a detective!

**T**HIS IS SALLY. She was able to buy a Seal. Do you know why? Can you hear the same "SSS" sound at the beginning of Sally and Seal?

This is Peter. He bought a Pony. Do you know why? Can you hear the same "PPP" sound at the beginning of Peter and Pony?

*NOW CAN YOU SOLVE THE PET SHOP MYSTERY?*

45

**D**onald wants to buy a D_____.

**F**rank would love to buy the F_____.

**S**ally hopes her mother will let her buy a S_____.

**B**illy has just the right amount of money to buy a B_____.

**M**ona wants the M_____.

**R**obert hopes he can buy the R_____.

**T**erry wants a T_____, but her mother says she can't have one.

Rabbit

Seal

Bird

Tiger

Fish

Monkey

Dog

*Were the children happy?*

..........Yes! Except for Terry. She couldn't buy a real Tiger, and she didn't want a Turtle, so she's going next door to the toy store. What do you think she'll buy? Why, a toy Tiger!

## More Ways to Play Along

1 Tell your child that the next day some more children went to the pet shop. See if he can think of animals these children might buy. Remind him that a child can buy any animal whose name begins with the same sound as that child's name.

Gale could buy a
Leo could buy a
Paul could buy a     (goat)     (lion)     (pig)

2 What would you buy at the pet shop? What sound begins your name? What could you buy at the toy store?

3 Read the picture captions again. Show your child that the capital letter at the beginning of each name is the same letter that begins the name of the proper animal. Teach him the names of the letters.

48

# Goldilocks

**Identifying sizes and shapes**

## How to Play Along

Whenever you see words printed in red, emphasize them. When you see the 🛑 ask your child to point to the correct picture.

I'm going to talk about all of the pictures as I read the story. Can you point to each picture as I mention it?

Once upon a time there were three bears—a **GREAT BIG FATHER BEAR** 🛑 — a **MIDDLE-SIZED MOTHER BEAR** 🛑 — and a **TEENY-TINY BABY BEAR** 🛑

49

They each had a round bowl for their porridge (porridge is another name for hot cereal), which they loved to eat for breakfast. Father Bear had a GREAT BIG BOWL ⬢, Mother Bear had a MIDDLE-SIZED BOWL ⬢, and Baby Bear had a TEENY-TINY BOWL ⬢

One morning they tasted their porridge and found it was too hot; so the three bears went for a walk while the porridge was cooling.

They had just left when a little girl, named Goldilocks, walked by the house. She peeped through the windows and knocked on the door. When nobody answered, she decided to tiptoe in and look around.

First she saw the THREE ROUND BOWLS OF PORRIDGE ⬢. "Umm, this looks good," she said. So she tasted the porridge in the GREAT BIG BOWL ⬢, but it was too hot. Then she tasted the porridge in the MIDDLE-SIZED BOWL ⬢, and it was also too hot. But when she tasted the porridge in the TEENY-TINY BOWL ⬢, it was just right, so she ate it all up!

Then she sat in an ENORMOUS, WIDE CHAIR ⬢, which belonged to Father Bear. It was too hard. Next she sat in an AVERAGE, MIDDLE-SIZED CHAIR ⬢, which belonged to Mother Bear. It was too soft. Finally, she sat in Baby Bear's WEE, NARROW CHAIR ⬢, and it was just right. But Goldilocks was too heavy for such a small chair. It began to creak and groan, and then with a bang the chair broke; and with a thump and a thud Goldilocks was thrown to the floor.

She picked herself up and climbed the stairs to the bedroom. There she saw THREE BEDS ⬢ First she lay down on Father Bear's HUGE, LONG BED ⬢ , but it was too hard. Next she lay down on Mother Bear's AVERAGE, MIDDLE-SIZED BED ⬢ , but that was too soft. Finally she lay down on Baby Bear's TEENY-TINY, SHORT BED ⬢ , and that was just right. So guess what she did. She fell sound asleep.

Pretty soon the bears came back from their walk, hungry as bears for breakfast. "Somebody has been eating my porridge," cried GREAT BIG FATHER BEAR ⬢

"Somebody's been eating my porridge," cried MIDDLE-SIZED MOTHER BEAR ⬢

"Somebody's been eating my porridge," cried TEENY-TINY BABY BEAR ⬢ , "and has eaten it all up!"

"Well!" roared Father Bear. "Somebody's been sitting in my ENORMOUS, WIDE CHAIR 🛑."

"And somebody's been sitting in my AVERAGE, MIDDLE-SIZED CHAIR 🛑," cried Mother Bear.

"And somebody's been sitting in my WEE, NARROW CHAIR 🛑," cried Baby Bear, "and has broken it all to pieces."

Then the three bears went upstairs. Father Bear roared again, "Somebody's been sleeping in my HUGE, LONG BED ⬣."

"And somebody's been sleeping in my AVERAGE, MIDDLE-SIZED BED ⬣," cried Mother Bear.

"And somebody's been sleeping in my TEENY-TINY, SHORT BED ⬣," cried Baby Bear, "and here she is!"

Goldilocks woke up. She saw three bears staring at her, and she got so frightened that she ran downstairs and out of the house as fast as her legs could carry her.

And you can bet that she never walked into anyone's house uninvited again!

## More Ways to Play Along

1  After you have read the story a few times, play a picture game. Using the illustrations in the story, ask your child to find the biggest of everything; the smallest. Then ask:

   a What is wide?
   b What is narrow?
   c What is long?
   d What is short?

2  See if your child can think of other things that are tall, middle-sized, short, wide, narrow, etc.

# Handy Andy

**Reinforcement
in telling left from right**

## How to Play Along

When you see the 🛑 after the word LEFT or RIGHT, stop and wait for your child to raise the correct hand. If he has trouble, help him by touching the correct hand yourself.

Every time I say the word LEFT, raise your left hand. Every time I say the word RIGHT, raise your right hand.

"ANDY, WILL YOU EVER be able to tell LEFT 🛑 from RIGHT 🛑?" cried his mother. For Andy was ready to go out to play with his LEFT 🛑 glove on his RIGHT 🛑 hand and his RIGHT 🛑 glove on his LEFT 🛑 hand. He even had his RIGHT 🛑 shoe on his LEFT 🛑 foot and his LEFT 🛑 shoe on his RIGHT 🛑 foot.

Poor Andy. He never seemed to get things straight. He tried, he really did. But it took him so long to figure out which was LEFT ⬢ and which was RIGHT ⬢ that usually it was too late by then to go outside and play.

Andy's mother tried to help him. She thought and thought. And then she thought again. Finally she had an idea. "Andy, she said, "bring me a book. Any book."

So Andy brought in a book.

Then she said, "Look at the front of the book and put your hands around the sides. You can see that one side is pasted shut . . . it's locked up tight. That's the LEFT ⬢ side, and your LEFT ⬢ hand is holding it.

"The other side of the book opens RIGHT ⬢ up. And the side that opens RIGHT ⬢ up is the RIGHT ⬢ side!"

"Oh!" cried Andy. "The LEFT ⬢ side of this book is locked up tight. But the pages open RIGHT ⬢ up, on the RIGHT ⬢ !"

"RIGHT ⬢ ," smiled his mother, "I mean, that's correct!"

And from then on, whenever Andy couldn't remember which hand was which, he would pick up a book, remember to look at the front of it, and say:

"The LEFT ⬢ side of every book
Is locked up tight,
But the pages open RIGHT ⬢ up,
on the RIGHT ⬢ !"

## More Ways to Play Along

1 Show your child how to place his hands around a book as Andy did. Repeat the rhyme for him.

2 Read the story again. This time, ask your child to hop on his left or right foot whenever he hears the word *left* or *right*.

# A Guide to Play Tools for Children

The stories in the Headstart Series were designed to help develop those skills basic to all other learning.

Your child's playtime, too, is a time of skill development. You can enrich those play hours by seeing that he is provided with a variety of materials. A "prepared environment," much like a well-stocked medicine cabinet, can contribute much to sparking your child's readiness.

## GAMES AND TOYS

There are excellent products that can help develop skills. Look for games and toys that are well-designed and built for lasting play value. Lasting play value means that the toy or game can be used over and over again in various ways; that it demands participation and creative thinking on the part of the child, rather than narrowly confining him to a repeated "controlled activity." Try to choose a variety that might include:

1. Construction materials: blocks, logs, building sets of plastic and metal shapes.
2. Toys to assemble: wooden trains, plastic cars, farm sets.
3. Puzzles: start with very simple puzzles, two to four large pieces, preferably of wood.
4. Dolls and doll furniture; boys as well as girls enjoy these.
5. Puppets; hand and finger puppets are preferable to marionettes with strings.
6. Learning tools:
    a. Magnetic boards with letters and numbers.
    b. Alphabet cards.
    c. Sewing cards.
    d. Games based on color identification.
    e. Dominoes.
    f. Lotto games with large clear pictures to be matched.
    g. Playing cards.

7. Coordination games: pick-up sticks, balancing games, throwing and tossing games, fitting shapes in matching holes, building rings on a pole to make a pyramid, hammering pegs into a board.

8. Art materials: large sheets of paper, crayons, watercolors, poster paints, clay, scissors, paste.

9. Musical instruments: xylophone, toy piano, rhythm instruments.

10. Miniatures: scaled-down models of animals; people in different occupations, such as milkman, fireman; common household objects; boats, autos, etc.

### AND IN YOUR CHILD'S ROOM OR PLAY AREA

1. A clock with a clear face.

2. Container to keep toys neat for easy use. Save tin cans, large boxes or cookie tins, shoe boxes to hold toys.

3. A child-sized chair and work table.

4. Growing or living things, such as plants, birds, fish, etc.

5. Books—books—books: Picture books, ABC books, storybooks, counting books—for you to read with your child until, and even after, he becomes a reader. The expense can be kept to a minimum if you use your public library; and regular library visits with your child can do much to develop a positive attitude toward reading.

6. Records: A collection of records for your child can help to stimulate his listening abilities, provide a quiet activity, and add to his general information. Often, playing a record at nap time or bedtime will help an overtired child "unwind."

# A Guide to Books for Parents

These are books which you may find helpful for further understanding and practical guidance of your child's development. The list was prepared in coordination with the Child Study Association of America.

### Backyard Games and Activities
By Sylvia Cassell, Harper & Row. Specific suggestions for outdoor fun.

### The Children's Bookshelf
Bantam Books. An excellent guide to more than 2,000 books for and about children prepared by the Child Study Association of America.

### Fun with the Kids
By Shari Lewis, Macfadden-Bartell. Practical play activities for indoors and out, for different seasons, and changes in weather.

### Growing Up with Science
By Marianne Besser, McGraw-Hill. Ways a parent can help stimulate his child's scientific curiosity starting with preschoolers.

### How to Help Your Child in School
By Mark and Lawrence K. Frank, Viking; also in paperback, New American Library. A description of the stages of growth and learning in children from preschool to junior high school.

### Parent's Guide to Children's Play and Recreation
By Alvin Schwartz, Collier Books.

### The Parent's Manual: A Guide to the Emotional Development of Young Children
By Anna M. Wolf, Ungar.

### Television—How to Use It Wisely with Children
By Josette Frank, Pamphlet #409 (25 cents), available by writing to Child Study Association of America, 9 East 89th Street, New York, N.Y.

### Tested Ways to Help Your Child Learn
By Virginia Burgess Warren, Prentice-Hall. Suggestions, games, activities to stimulate learning in a variety of subjects.

### Two to Six: Suggestions for Parents and Teachers of Young Children
By Rose H. Alschuler & Assoc., Morrow. A handbook on child care, with advice on toys, books, music, play materials, etc.

### Your Child's Reading
By Josette Frank, Doubleday. How to guide the content of your child's reading and develop his interest in books.

### Your Child Steps Out
By Edgar S. Bley, Sterling. Preparing your child for various "first experiences."